PARIS AS IT WAS

Caged Nightingales. There have always been street markets of every kind in Paris. Around 1900, the period known as *'la Belle Epoque'*, or the Good Old Days, cage birds, often taken from the wild, were on sale every Sunday on the Ile de la Cité, near the cathedral of Notre-Dame, on the site of what was, during the week, the flower market. Birds and flowers go together in Paris. Nowadays, there is a poultry and bird market on the Quai de la Mégisserie, between the Pont Neuf and the Pont au Change.

PARIS AS IT WAS

by

J. B. WRIGHT

Photographs by

PAUL DESOYE

*'God invented the Parisian to prevent foreigners
from ever understanding anything about the French.'*

Alexandre Dumas fils

Front cover: *Place de la Concorde.*   On the right of the photograph
can be seen the Luxor column which was given to King Louis-
Philippe by Mohammed Ali, and had once stood before the great
temple of Thebes.

HENDON PUBLISHING : NELSON

ISBN: 0 86067 105 4

First published in Great Britain 1985 by
Hendon Publishing Co. Ltd.
Hendon Mill
Nelson
Lancashire
BB9 8AD

Printed in Great Britain by
Fretwell & Brian Ltd.
Goulbourne Street
Keighley
West Yorkshire
BD21 1PZ

*This book is dedicated to
all lovers of Paris and to
the memory of Paul Desoye*

INTRODUCTION

THE period covered by the photographs in this book, the thirty years between the 1890s and the 1920s, may seem no more than a heartbeat in the two thousand-year life of Paris, but in terms of significant events and artistic achievement it outshines many a whole century. During the nineties, the French Republic, still only a generation old, was shaken by anarchist bomb attacks, in one of which the President of the Republic was himself killed; numerous political scandals; and the Dreyfus affair, the spy case of the age. The very survival of the regime seemed in doubt. The remainder of the period was dominated by the First World War, with its five and a half million French casualties. Yet these years witnessed one of the most extraordinary manifestations of creativity ever known, for this is the era of artists like Cézanne, Gauguin, Toulouse-Lautrec, Monet, Renoir and Picasso; of composers like Debussy and Ravel, and of a whole galaxy of great writers. It was also the time when Paris, the undisputed pleasure capital of the universe, acquired the 'naughty' reputation it has kept. (The immediate reaction of most English people to the name 'Paris' is still 'Oo, là, là!').

In a physical sense, too, Paris reached a peak during these years, with the population of the city proper rising from 2,350,000 in 1886 to 2,800,000 in 1921, then falling to the present-day level of less than 2,200,000. The movement is outwards, to the suburbs, the population of which has increased from some 80,000 at the beginning of last century to 6,500,000 in the 1980s.

Throughout these years, the British came to Paris in droves, as they still do, by exactly the same land–sea routes. Last century, according to the 1888 Baedeker, the journey London–Paris, via Boulogne, took '14–17 hours, exclusive of detention in Boulogne, where the trains do not correspond.' By the 1920s, it had been reduced to 6–7 hours, and an air service — Croydon–Le Bourget, in three hours — was in operation.

Except for the President of the Republic and the Dutch royal couple, making their single appearance, the people these photographs catch in a moment of Parisian time move in the margins of history, doing the things people do regardless of the political weather: taking days off; wearing their best clothes on high days and holidays; bussing it to the shops; enjoying the moods of their city. As they pass, and one gets to know them better, two contrasting French views come to mind of these Parisians at home, with their legendary wit and street-wisdom. According to a recent writer : 'The Parisian isn't the eighth wonder of the world, but the commonplace product of the kind of life found in all big cities.' On the other hand, in the sixteenth century Michel de Montaigne declared : 'I love Paris tenderly — even its warts and blemishes. I only feel French through this great city, great in its people and its location, the glory of France, and one of the noblest ornaments of the world.'

The aim of this book is to convert you, if you need conversion, to the opinion of Montaigne.

J. B. Wright
1985

BIRDS, BEASTS and FLOWERS

Bird Market.   Another view of the bird market, with a young hawker of chickweed and bird-seed in the foreground. The cage bird and the pot of flowers are features of most Paris homes. Birds were then given fancy names like 'widows with gold necklaces'; 'high-fliers from St Helena'; 'young Popes'; and 'Bengalis from Bombay able to yodel'. Up to 1860, when there was an immense clearance, this was one of the most ill-famed quarters of Paris.

Horse Show, Champ de Mars.   The location is unmistakable : beyond the Eiffel Tower, opened in 1889, are the Seine, and one tower of the Trocadéro Palace, built for the 1878 Universal Exhibition, and pulled down to make way for the present Palais de Chaillot, which dates from the Exhibition of 1937. Though the car had made its appearance, it still seemed inconceivable that it would ever replace the horse. In her memoirs, the Countess de Pange records that of the fourteen servants of her mother's household in 1910, a coachman and several grooms were needed to look after the five horses.

Riding in the Bois.   The Bois de Boulogne, which covers an area of over 2,200 acres, takes its name from a church founded by pilgrims from the seaport of Boulogne-sur-Mer. Since Napoleon I, all French rulers have contributed to its embellishment. The last kings (1815–1848) even hunted in it, though in such a confined space, with the beaters sometimes outnumbering the game, there was little sport to be had. Bought by the city of Paris in 1852, it was provided with lakes, islands and waterfalls. The 'Rotten Row' of the Bois is the Allée de Longchamp, but there are other places, like this one, where horses may be ridden.

Flower Market.   It was here that the widowed Marie-Antoinette's jailers would come in the late summer and early autumn of 1793 to buy flowers for the cell of the nearby Conciergerie in which the Queen awaited execution. (At least, this is what they claimed in 1814, when France was again a monarchy.) Then as now, the site is dominated by the Tour de l'Horloge (Clock Tower), which was totally rebuilt in 1853, around the sixteenth-century clock: compared with London, Paris has very few public clocks — this is certainly the oldest.

Omnibus driver. Rudyard Kipling knew the Paris of 1878 as a schoolboy. In one of his last books, *Souvenirs of France,* he remembered 'the ribaldly inquisitive cabmen of those days', how 'they talked too much, those gentlemen in the leather hats'. From them, he picked up a lot of bad (French) language. A race apart, they were devoted to their horses, with whom they spent long days and nights, in all weathers. Already, the petrol engine had doomed them to extinction.

Students' Carnival. Since the publication in 1851 of *Scènes de la Vie de Bohème* (Bohemian Life) by Henri Murger, which later inspired operas by Puccini and Leoncavallo, art students in Paris have been expected to be boisterous, witty and shocking. This group of students from the Paris Ecole des Beaux Arts (School of Fine Arts) are clearly doing their best to live up to their reputation by this display of scurrilous and satirical posters, some of which are definitely not nice.

Mid-Lent Carnival.   Today, the only public holidays permitted by law in France are New Year's Day; Easter Monday; 1st May; Ascension Day; Whit Monday; 14 July (Bastille Day); and Christmas. Eighty years ago, not only was the end of Lent celebrated, but also the fact that the dreary fasting-time was half over. The procession is moving towards the Seine, with the Paris Town Hall, razed to the ground during the 1871 civil war (Commune of Paris), and later rebuilt, on its left. The Town Hall Square shown here was, until 1802, known as the Place de Grève : it was the place of execution for common law criminals.

The Fair at Neuilly.   Neuilly-sur-Seine lies just outside the Paris city limits, along the northern edge of the Bois de Boulogne. The annual Fête de Neuilly, or Neuilly Fair, is held between mid-June and mid-July, and is a favourite summer excursion for Parisians. The straw hat (*canotier*) worn by the man on the left belongs very much to the period : it later became inseparable from the stage persona of Maurice Chevalier. The basket-work frames of the dodgem cars remind us that we are still in the age of the bath-chair.

First Communion.   A red-letter day in the life of every young girl of the time. Sixty years afterwards, a Frenchwoman who had made her first communion in 1900 wrote : 'Getting up early, and going out breakfastless, were adventures in themselves. I was even forbidden to clean my teeth for fear of breaking my fast by swallowing a drop of water. My mother gave me the usual gold watch, and I also received splendidly-bound, but unreadable, books full of pious illustrations.'

Palm Sunday.　Gendarmes look on benevolently, while what could be a whole family offer *buis* (box twigs) for sale at the entrance to a Paris church. In France, this greenery is still as closely associated with Palm Sunday as the lily of the valley (*muguet*) with the First of May. Note the VIII on the tunic of the right-hand gendarme : this means that he is attached to the 8th *arrondissement,* or district, of Paris — the very heart of the capital situated between the Place de la Concorde and the Arc de Triomphe.

State Primary School.   When the Third French Republic was established in 1870 — the First followed the overthrow of the monarchy in 1793; the Second flourished briefly in 1848; the Third came to an end in 1940, and the Fourth in 1958 — high priority was given to the introduction of a uniform state system of education, as a means of winning support for the new regime, adopted because it was 'the regime that divides us least'. It is still as centralised as ever, and the story goes that at any given moment the Minister for Education knows exactly which page of which textbook is being turned in schools like this throughout France.

Street Works I. Until the arrival of Baron Haussmann, Prefect of the Seine 1853–1870, Paris was still largely a mediaeval city. Then, in the words of the novelist Emile Zola : 'Paris was slashed with sabre-cuts, and disappeared in a cloud of plaster.' After Haussmann, there was little large-scale activity until the 1960s, when the first tower blocks began to punctuate the Paris sky-line. Pictured here is no heroic effort of that kind, but nevertheless intensely interesting to local residents, who are grouped around, no doubt commenting volubly.

Street Works II.   Carts bringing raw materials for street repairs were also the responsibility of the Prefect of the Seine, an official nominated by the government with wide powers affecting many aspects of Parisian life. It was he, ultimately, who would have caused these carts containing road-mending materials to be filled and driven to their destination. The use of petrol-driven transport was still very patchy, though taxis, like the one with the barrel-shaped bonnet shown here, were already ousting the fiacres and other horse-drawn passenger carriages.

The President of the Republic on Duty. Wilhelmina was Queen of the Netherlands from 1898 to 1948, when she abdicated in favour of her daughter, Juliana (who herself abdicated in favour of her daughter, Beatrice, in 1980). Here Wilhelmina is seen with her Consort on a state visit to France, accompanied by the then French head of state, Raymond Poincaré, President. 1913–1920. The Netherlands maintained its neutrality during the First World War — and gave asylum to Kaiser Wilhelm II after it — despite assiduous wooing by both sides. This state visit may have been linked with a French attempt to induce the Dutch to make common cause with the Allies.

LEISURE

Sunday in the Tuileries Gardens.   The royal palace of the Tuileries was created in the sixteenth century on the site of a tile-works — hence the name. For three centuries, it was occupied by successive French sovereigns before being burnt down during the last days of the Commune of Paris, in May 1871. Painted by Manet and Monet, the gardens were a popular place for Sunday outings. In 1900, the French President of the day, Emile Loubet, invited 22,000 mayors from France and Algeria to have lunch with him there : the tables placed end to end would have stretched for five miles.

Sunday walk : rue de l'Abreuvoir, Montmartre. Until it officially became part of Paris in 1860, Montmartre — the Martyrs' Mount — led the existence of a small independent village. It was then discovered and over-run by the artists' colony, and in the 1870s became the site of a major construction project : the building of the Basilica of the Sacred Heart (Sacré-Coeur), which can be seen at the end of this little street. It is said that, because of the immense solidity of its foundations — 83 columns of masonry penetrating to a depth of more than a hundred feet — even if the hill of Montmartre were removed, the Basilica would still be left standing.

Start of Paris Marathon. From the birth of the internal combustion engine, French cars were as technically advanced as any. The great names of the French car industry, Louis Renault (1877–1944), and André Citroën (1878–1935) were almost exact contemporaries. Their early achievements belong to the *Belle Epoque*, and were trumpeted by such pioneer specialist magazines as *L'Auto*, which used all the publicity resources then available to boost its sales. Not only did *L'Auto* organise some of the first city marathons, as pictured here, it is also credited with promoting the one and only marathon swim in the Seine.

Coaches and Four.   One went driving in the Bois de Boulogne to take the air, and be seen. Though the horse was still supreme, the first automobiles were already about, and at what was known as the Chalet du Cycle people — including ladies in voluminous bloomers — could hire bicycles and explore the remoter parts of the Bois. Though the centuries before the invention of the automobile are often thought of as the golden age of the pedestrian, it's worth remembering that Louis-Sebastien Mercier, in his *Picture of Paris* (1781), was already complaining about the two hundred fatal coach accidents which happened every year.

Palais-Royal Gardens. The Palais-Royal was built by Cardinal Richelieu in the seventeenth century, and bequeathed by him to King Louis XIII. It later became the property of the Orleans branch of the royal family. Ransacked during the revolution of 1848, and burnt during the Commune of 1871, it was rebuilt in the 1870s. The gardens, with their lime-trees and central fountain, date from the 1780s, and have been lively with children ever since. The surrounding buildings are an imitation of the Piazza San Marco in Venice. There are two notable statues : one by Rodin of the poet Victor Hugo, the other of Camille Desmoulins, who made a famous speech here at a crucial moment of the French Revolution.

Off to the Races. The form of transport is a charabanc, which comes from the French word *char à bancs*, meaning 'car with seats'. The word has hardly survived the horse-drawn era, but in the twenties and thirties we were still referring to what we now call 'coaches' — another survival from horse-transport — as 'charabancs'. This party might be going to the races either at Longchamp (flat-racing), situated between the Seine and the Bois de Boulogne, or to Auteuil (steeplechasing), to the east of the Bois. These were the days before the *tiercé*, the triple chance, which now has all France on tenterhooks over the week-end.

Hunting Expedition.   The right to shoot almost anything that moves was one of those acquired during the French Revolution of 1789, and none is more appreciated or exercised. When the season opens, groups like these set out to the remoter corners of the Ile-de-France, and much ammunition is expended. Because the French are an eminently practical people, all hunting is for the pot. What other national cuisine boasts dishes like 'Larks in breadcrust' and 'sweet and sour wild boar'?

Booksellers' Stalls.   E. V. Lucas once wrote : 'The Seine has a mile of old book and curiosity stalls, whereas the Thames has nothing'. The open-air booksellers of Paris — known as *bouquinistes* — first installed themselves on the Pont Neuf. When they were cleared off the bridge in 1650, they set up shop on the parapets of the quays of the Seine, where they have been to this day. There are now more mass-produced tourist items than first editions, but you really never know what you are going to find.

STREET SCENES

Paris 1900.   A panorama of the Paris of the central year of the *Belle Epoque*, with the Great Wheel of the Exhibition of that year to the left of the Eiffel Tower. One little girl who visited the Exhibition remembered sixty years later a primitive kind of moving staircase which filled everyone with terror; an aepyornis egg, and models of prehistoric monsters, still called 'antediluvian'. The two avenues, Iéna, named after a Napoleonic victory, and Kléber, after one of Napoleon's marshals, ran from the Etoile to, respectively, the Iéna bridge over the Seine, and the Trocadéro palace (demolished in 1937), visible on the right.

The 1910 Flood in the rue de Bièvre.   In the early years of the century, the Seine overflowed its banks several times, notably in October 1910, when this photograph was taken. The soldier was on duty three-quarters of a century ago to prevent looting; today, you will find gendarmes manning a checkpoint at about the same spot to monitor comings and goings outside the Paris home of President Mitterand, which is in the rue de Bièvre. The street's name is that of the rivulet which, until the formation of the first Paris water company in 1789, was the only reliable source for the households of the Left Bank.

Picturesque Montmartre I.   Montmartre can be reached from the plain by a short funicular railway — so short that, per metre, it offers probably the most expensive journey in the world — but most people prefer to toil up the various flights of stairs. The centre of the village is the Place du Tertre, a gigantic tourist trap, full of minor artists and surrounded by restaurants. Montmartre still has its own vineyard, and many picturesque houses; but the clearances shown here have been filled by numerous blocks of flats which frequently spoil the rustic atmosphere so sedulously cultivated.

Picturesque Montmartre II.   Montmartre, 330 feet above the Seine, is a place of hills completely dominating Paris and its plain, a fact which all armies seeking to attack or occupy the capital have recognised. These heights saw the final struggle between Napoleon's armies and the Prussian and Russian allies on 30 March 1814, as well as the beginnings of the civil war of 1871. It was artillery based on Montmartre which shelled Paris and the Communards during their last stand in May 1871.

Mistletoe Sellers.   Another irruption of the countryside into central Paris. Mistletoe in France has
associations with Christmas, but more as a bringer of good luck to the household than as an excuse for
kissing the girls. Not much luck seems to have rubbed off on to this man and his son : the passing
bourgeois look as if they might be thinking : 'Why waste time on such ragamuffins?' One hopes that
the boy did not survive his difficult childhood only to die in some First World War blood-bath.

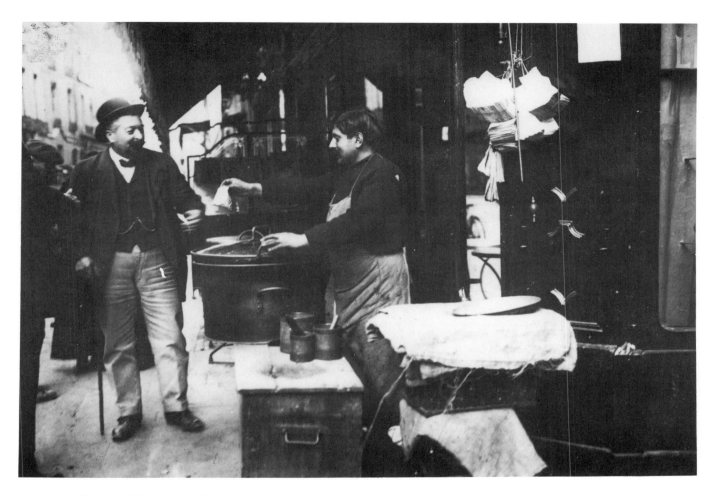

Chestnut Vendors I.   France is a major producer of chestnuts (*marrons*): in some districts, such as Creuse, Limousin, Haute-Vienne and Corsica, they are a staple article of diet, whether eaten raw, boiled, stewed or grilled. They are also used extensively in the classical French cuisine, and in sweets and pastries. But in Paris the most popular source is the street trader, here seen with all his equipment. Later, perhaps, the customer in the billycock hat will buy some *marrons glacés,* or have some chestnut Mont-Blanc as his dinner dessert.

Chestnut Vendors II. A little knot of street-vendors, among them another chestnut-seller. Though unconnected with the café, they profit from the shelter of its awning. Note the prices for coffee with milk, hot chocolate and beer (15 centiemes a tankard), also the *belle époque* ironwork above the chestnut man's head, and the cap worn by the pipe-smoking man in the centre of the group to the left. This is the universal workman's cap of the time : there are several photographs of Lenin wearing one.

Boulevard de Clichy.   This artery, named after a village now swallowed up in Paris, is at the base of the hill of Montmartre. The little girl's dress, the cobblestones, and the horse-cab hark back to the *Belle Epoque*, but in the foreground are the petrol-driven omnibuses which were already helping to give Paris traffic its special quality. The photograph seems to have been taken at the witching hour of noon, or thereabouts, when the whole of Paris knocks off for lunch, and the rest of France follows suit.

Rue du Chevalier de la Barre. Near the Sacré-Coeur in Montmartre, this street was known as rue des Rosiers when, in March 1871, two generals were shot against the wall of the garden of no. 36 by a crowd resisting the transfer of artillery from Montmartre to Paris. This was the spark that set off the two-month civil war during which somewhere between 20,000 and 40,000 Frenchmen were killed. The Chevalier de la Barre was a young nobleman executed in 1766 for failing to show proper respect at a religious ceremony; the renaming of the street was thus an anti-clerical counterblast to the pervasive piety of the Sacré-Coeur.

Rue Brise-Miche.   The name of the street means 'break-bread', a *miche* being a large round loaf. Only the name now remains of this ancient street which, when the photograph was taken, was full of varied activity : hotels, wine-shops and locksmiths. It's part of one of the oldest quarters of Paris, the Marais (literally, Marsh) which has lately been invaded by the ultra-modern, British-designed arts centre known as the Centre Pompidou. Walk up the rue Brise-Miche, and there it is, with its working parts hanging out!

Rue de Lyon.   This street runs between the Place de la Bastille — the monument to the 380 victims of the Revolution of 1830, marking the site of the Bastille prison, stormed by the mob on 14 July 1789, can be seen on the left — and the Gare de Lyon. It was to provide access to this railway station that the street was opened in 1847, a forerunner of the grand clearance of old Paris, and of the building boom which followed, during the twenty years of the Second Empire (1852–1870).

Rue de la Paix. This elegant street, named after the European peace of 1814, which was immediately followed by the bloody Waterloo campaign of 1815, connects the Place de l'Opéra and the Place Vendôme, whose column bearing a statue of Napoleon I can be seen in the centre background. One of the last acts of the Commune of Paris, threatened with extinction by the advancing government troops, was to overthrow the column. It was in the rue de la Paix that the legendary English fashion designer, Charles Frederick Worth, established his first business.

Boulevard Richard-Lenoir.   Connecting the Place de la Bastille and the Boulevard Voltaire, and named after the eighteenth-century manufacturer, and his partner, Lenoir — as one might say Crosse & Blackwell Street — this is an area so solidly middle class that when Simenon wished to emphasise the bourgeois quality of his Inspector Maigret, he situated his apartment here. To this day, many Parisian streets have open-air markets, but most cater for daily food needs. Junk like this, and many other kinds, is now mostly concentrated at the flea market near the Porte de Clignancourt métro station.

Office Workers Queuing to Go Home.   We think our rush hours hard to bear, but imagine horse-drawn vehicles added to the mix of buses, cars and pedestrians. Eighty years ago, the French worked longer hours than we do, and in the private sector still do : this would be lateish on a summer evening. Note the characteristic shape of the taxi's bonnet. It was taxis like these that were used in 1914 to transfer French army units to a point threatened by the advancing German armies, with decisive results on the outcome of the crucial battle of the Marne.

Gathering of the Trams. Trams have vanished from Paris just as they have from London : these belong to the days when the smell of horses mingled with the reek of petrol fumes on the *grands boulevards*. As the grey winter afternoon thickens in, reinforcements are brought up for the evening rush hour to take passengers as far afield as Montrouge, one of the southernmost districts of Paris, and, like Montmartre, not incorporated in the city until 1860. In the *Belle Epoque*, Montrouge was noted for its market-gardens.

FOOD and DRINK

Street Carts.   Carts were the light vans of 1900 Paris. They were used not only to move produce from the central market to individual shops and restaurants, but also as kerbside stalls. Supplies of vegetables like these would come from the gardens of suburbs like Nanterre, where the enormous tower block known as La Défense now stands, to the central market. There, transport of all kinds would be waiting to distribute them throughout Paris. Note the middle-class bowler counterpointing the workman's cap.

Barrow-girl. This lady is selling some of the famous salads of the Ile-de-France, the region to the west of Paris, which will have arrived at the central market, Les Halles, at three or four o'clock in the morning. She will have collected her barrowful of curly lettuce a little later : she hopes that by lunch time it will all have gone. The price she is charging is low, but so are wages and the cost of living : a meal in the best restaurant in Paris would cost only 10 francs, just forty times what she is charging for a half a kilo of lettuce.

Auvergnat Restaurant.   Since the sixteenth century, there has been a constant migration of people from the Auvergne, the mountainous region in central France — known as Auvergnats, or, more vulgarly, Auverpins — to Paris and other large towns. After a few years in the city, working as masons, carpenters and labourers, they would go home to get married, return for the rest of their working life, then finally retire to their native village. Auvergnat specialities served here might include the *potée*, a soup made with vegetables and pork; thrush cutlets, and jellied eels.

Restaurant du Coucou. This was one of the famous restaurants of Montmartre at the turn of the century, specialising in Italian dishes. (The restaurant is still there, in the same building, but the *Coucou* — cuckoo — has become the *Plumeau*, or feather-duster. Whether the new name is a reference to the cruel fate of the original cuckoo is not known.) Around 1900, Montmartre was the most prestigious night spot of Paris, with the restaurants being celebrated either for their cooking or their cabaret. It was unusual for a restaurant to excel in both departments.

Les Halles.   The old central market, or *Halles Centrales*, was one of the great monuments of Paris for nearly 120 years. Built of cast iron and glass during the Second Empire, it finally — like Covent Garden in London — became too out-dated and inconvenient, and in 1969 was transferred to Rungis, near Orly airport, leaving a notorious *Trou* (hole) behind, which is only just being filled with new buildings. It consisted of twelve pavilions, one for each of the various kinds of produce, from salads to river fish, from meat and poultry to cheese. It was Covent Garden, Billingsgate, Leadenhall and Smithfield rolled into one. No wonder Zola wrote a novel in praise of it. (*Le Ventre de Paris*, or 'The Belly of Paris'.)

Halle aux Vins. The wine market, always separate from the central market, was originally established in 1644, but its great period began when Napoleon I made it a tax-free zone. The main structure was completed by 1818, and by the time it was enlarged fifty years later its 69 cellars were capable of storing 160,000 hectolitres of brandy alone. It was nearly obliterated by bombing in 1944, and not rebuilt. The site is now occupied by buildings of the Science Faculty of the University of Paris, overflowing from the rue de Jussieu.

GETTING ABOUT

Early Traffic Signals. These solid cast-iron constructions, long since demolished, were the first non-automatic traffic signals. Not only were they a serious attempt to bring some order to the chaotic traffic conditions of the time — and the first realisation that the onset of the automobile age had created totally novel problems — but they also offered the gendarme inside, who worked the controls, a shelter against the vagaries of the Paris weather. Note the Folies Bergère sign on the left : this famous music-hall is in the rue Richer to the east of the rue du Faubourg-Montmartre.

Ballooning. Ballooning has had strong links with Paris ever since the first ascents of the Montgolfier brothers, the inventors (1783) of the hot-air balloon. In 1870, during the siege of Paris by the German Army, it was the only way of maintaining contact with the outside world : during this period, the world's first airmail postal service was developed. The balloons were kept in the Place St-Pierre, at the foot of the hill where the Sacré-Coeur now is. In charge of them was the photographer Nadar, who appears in Jules Verne's novel *From the Earth to the Moon* as Michael Ardan.

Montparnasse Station I. On 22 October 1895, a locomotive jumped the buffers at Montparnasse station — which serves western France, i.e. Brittany and the Atlantic Coast — and burst through the station façade to emerge on the Place de Rennes, as pictured here. On 24 September 1900, the brakes failed on a train coming from Versailles. Again the engine went through the buffers, but came to rest on the top step of the main staircase. Why it was only Montparnasse station that was plagued by such accidents during this period is one of the many mysteries of Paris.

Montparnasse Station II.   Since Montparnasse station serves Brittany, it's logical that its square, the Place de Rennes, should be named after the region's capital. The station dates from 1852, and the line it serves forms the boundary between the 14th and 15th *arrondissements*, after crossing the avenue du Maine, the starting-point of the old stage-coach route to the western provinces. To raise the new station to the same level as an older one in the avenue du Maine, tons of soil had to be brought to the site to be bricked in with containing walls.

St-Lazare Station. The Western Station, Gare St-Lazare, has the largest suburban traffic of any Parisian station, serving such districts as Asnières, Argenteuil and Versailles — it is the capital's main commuter station. During the Franco-Prussian War of 1870–1, it was used as a hospital. Note the shoe-shine stand claiming to operate 'Vite et Bien' (Quick and Well), and the domed column for posters. The Splendid restaurant was a stone's throw from the station : for an extra half-franc, you could have entertainment with your dinner.

Horse-drawn Trams. Another view of the Place de Rennes, taken from the entrance to Montparnasse station. Note the itinerary of the horse-drawn tram. Starting at the Place de la Bastille, it crossed the Seine by the Pont d'Austerlitz, and connected with three Paris railway stations, serving respectively the west (Montparnasse); the south (Lyon); and the Orléans network (Orléans), with halts at the Gobelins, since 1662 the state tapestry workshops, and the Observatory, home since 1919 of the International Time Bureau, the ultimate world authority on the measurement of time.

Horse-drawn Omnibus I.   In its heyday, there were 34 different horse-drawn omnibus lines crossing Paris in every direction from 7 a.m. to midnight. At many points, an omnibus passed every four minutes. Apart from a few owned by the French railway authority, they all belonged to the Compagnie Générale des Omnibus. At the time this photograph was taken, there were two types in use — the old type, of which this one is a specimen, with two horses, and places for 26 people (14 inside), and the newer model, with three horses, and seating for 40.

Horse-drawn Omnibus II.   A view of the newer, three-horse, 40-seater omnibus, developed from the model pictured in the previous photograph. The driver, wearing the leather hat with the white band which is the badge of his trade, is covered from the waist downwards : otherwise, he has to endure whatever unpleasantness the Paris weather has in store. Note that the discovery of the great publicity value of advertisements on public transport had yet to be made.

Horse-drawn Omnibus III.   Vincennes, with its forest and chateau, lies to the east of Paris, just outside the city limits. It used to be the site of a major omnibus station, from which the old two-horse buses descended on Paris. The two lines shown here plied between the Panthéon, where the illustrious dead of France are buried, and the fashionable Parc de Monceau district, and from Montsouris, where there is a pleasant park containing a reproduction of the palace of the Bey of Tunis — opposite the park is now the University City, where students from all over the world are accommodated — to the Place de la République.

Coach and Four in the Bois de Boulogne. The Bois was once described by an English writer as 'Hyde Park, Kempton Park and Epping Forest all thrown together between Shepherd's Bush, Acton and the river.' It has two lakes, the Lower Lake (Lac Inférieur) and Higher Lake (Lac Supérieur), and two racecourses, Longchamp and Auteuil. There are restaurants too — a famous one in 1900 was near the waterfall — and a zoo (Jardin d'Acclimatation). In the great days of the horse, the fashion being set by the Emperor Napoleon III and his Empress, Eugénie, it was an incomparable spot for showing off a spanking coach and four.

Gendarme No. 22. The French police — here represented by a resplendent 'PC 22' — are in general the responsibility of the Ministry of the Interior, though in the countryside, where they are known as the *Gendarmerie Nationale*, they come under the Ministry for the Armed Forces. Such features of the present-day police force as the Compagnies Republicaines de Sécurité (Republican Security Companies, or heavily-armed riot squads, of which there are currently about sixty) were unknown in the *Belle Epoque.*

Early Petrol Omnibuses I. These machines posed many problems — though Paris, with its wide avenues and boulevards created during the Second Empire, largely to facilitate the rapid deployment of troops, was better prepared for the advent of the internal combustion engine than most capitals — and their general resemblance to agricultural equipment was enhanced by the watering-cans used to cool their constantly overheating radiators. They had two classes : the front part was First, and the rear portion and platform (where smoking was allowed) Second. Each route was divided into two or three sections, and for city routes tickets were sold in strips or booklets (carnets), available at tobacconists' and certain kiosks.

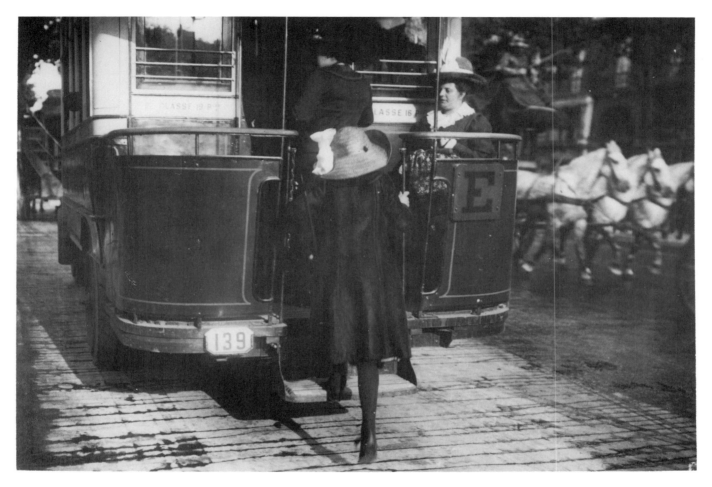

Early Petrol Omnibuses II. Very much of its time, when it seemed as if horse-drawn transport would always remain a serious competitor, passengers entered this single-decker bus from the rear platform, while the double-decker horse-drawn bus visible on the left has stairs leading to the upper level, which was usually uncovered. The buses serving the main city routes bore letters of identification : this is Line E (Madeleine–Bastille), running the whole length of the boulevards as far as the Place de la Bastille.

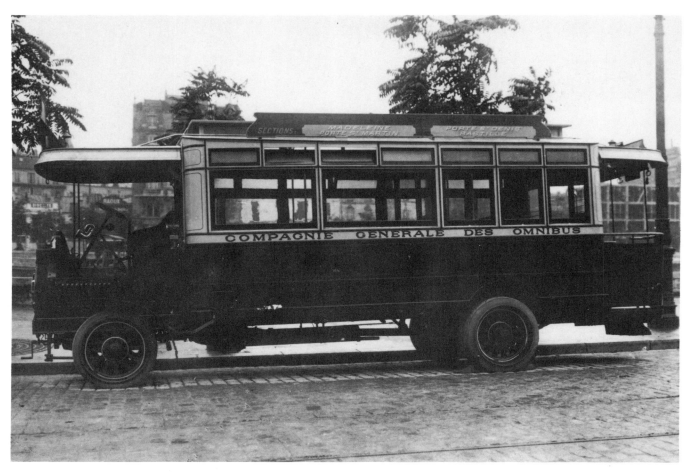

Early Petrol Omnibuses III.   A typical early machine, complete with bulb-horn and starting handle. Passengers got on at the rear, and the driver swathed himself in rugs and tarpaulins. At the outbreak of war in 1939, Paris had three thousand such buses, only slightly modified over the years. Under the German occupation, no more than a thousand were allowed to circulate at any one time, the remainder being kept in reserve 'for contingencies'. Buses from the reserve were used for the *Grande Rafle* (Great Raid) of July 1942, when 20,000 Paris Jews were rounded up before being shipped off to Germany and the concentration camps.

Early Petrol Omnibuses IV.　　Another view of the early omnibus with its solid tyres and rear platform bulging with passengers. Note the small boy in his sailor suit, an English fashion widely copied in France, and the noble feather in the hat of the lady with him. The bus driver, well-wrapped up in his open cab, waits for the gendarme — standing fearlessly in the middle of the road — to give the signal to move, while the man in the boater on the left profits from the halt to cross the street, without benefit of the still-to-be-invented pedestrian crossing.

Traffic Jam : Palais-Royal.   We have now moved from fully horse-drawn traffic, through a mixture of horses and petrol-engines, to fully-mechanised transport, though buses and taxis still outnumber private cars. This particular traffic jam happened at the Palais-Royal, behind the Louvre Museum. At that time, the Hotel du Louvre, seen here, was a first-class hotel, but with a tariff about half that of the most famous Paris hotels, such as the Ritz, the Crillon, the Meurice and the George V. Like all Paris hotels under the German occupation, the Louvre was requisitioned : it is now called the Louvre-Concorde.

PERIOD PIECES

The Duel.   Duelling came back into fashion in the 1890s : there was even a club where those who knew nothing about sword-play, or were simply scared stiff, could hire professional substitutes. In some public places, a glance, or chance remark, was enough to bring about the despatch of seconds, and the dawn confrontation. A well-known duelling ground was the casino on La Grande Jatte, an island in the Seine between Neuilly and Courbevoie, magnificently painted in the 1880s by Georges Seurat. Here 'satisfaction' was obtained for real or imagined insults, and political and personal scores settled.

Aviation exhibition.   France was among the leading aviation pioneers, and the first French Aviation Exhibition in December 1908 was a notable event in the history of manned flight. It was held in the Grand Palais, and according to one observer brought together 'everything thought capable, in reality and in dreams, of taking to the air.' In May 1909, was inaugurated the world's first aerodrome, at Juvisy, in the Ile-de-France, while on 25 July the same year Blériot flew from Calais to Dover, and in August was held the Grand International Aviation Week at Rheims. France was on the path that would lead to the Caravelle and Mystère aircraft of our day.

Fashion II. The period 1909–1910 was one of the great turning points in womens' fashions. Among other social developments, the suffragette movement brought a new emphasis on the natural unrestricted figure, and the clutter and fussiness of earlier fashions fell into disfavour. Among the new designs was the tailored suit, as shown here : by 1905, this was acceptable street wear. Even the overblown *belle époque* hat was temporarily discarded in favour of something simpler, and to our eyes, much more elegant.

Fashion III. The Grand Prix de Paris, which these ladies have gathered to see, or be been at, was one of the great dates of the Parisian social calendar. It was run at Longchamp race-course towards the end of June, and was the signal for high society to leave the capital for the sea-side : nobody who was anybody could afford to be seen in Paris after that date. The fashions here belong to the period 1912–13, when skirts were tubular, with scarves and sashes arranged vertically. The hat was back with a vengeance, at new high levels of fantasy.

Fashion IV. It was said of some of the more breathtakingly elegant Parisiennes that 'their mothers conceived them by swallowing a pearl.' The sort of vibration that sets them apart can be produced by a detail of dress, or an almost divine rightness about the whole appearance, as in this photograph. The fashion here would be about 1913, when turban shapes and toques were popular. Note that the ankles can now be seen, revealing high laced, or buttoned, shoes, made of kid, suede or gabardine, with high heels and pointed toes.

Fashion V. One of the great fashion designers of the period, Paul Poiret, drew inspiration from oriental sources, and from the colours and costumes of the Russian ballet, the sensation of 1909. These ladies are wearing kimono-style jackets which might have been designed by Poiret; also on view is one of the elaborate parasols of the time, made of silk, lace (or chiffon), edged with ruffles and trimmed with velvet ribbon. The large hats stuck with ostrich plumes were a revival of the 'Gainsborough' style.

PLACES

Place de L'Opéra.   In area, the Paris Opera is the largest theatre in the world. After barely surviving an assassination attempt outside the old opera house, Napoleon III decreed that it, and its gloomy approaches, should be replaced : hence the present structure, designed by Charles Garnier. Though the foundation stone was laid in 1862, it was not inaugurated until 1875. During the German occupation of 1940–44, the German Kommandantur, where Parisians had to apply for passes and authorisations of all kinds, was situated just to the right of the Opera.

Pont au Change.   A view of one of the Seine bridges, the Pont au Change (rebuilt in 1858–9) with, in the background, left to right, the column and fountain marking the site of the Châtelet prison, and the Sarah Bernhardt theatre. Behind the theatre, which the actress leased in 1899, is the St-Jacques tower, all that remains of the sixteenth-century church of St-Jacques-de-la-Boucherie, after the demolitions of the 1789 revolution. During the German occupation, the name of the Jewess Sarah Bernhardt, who died in 1923, had to be removed.

Pont St-Michel.   The Pont St-Michel is one of the five bridges linking the Ile de la Cité with the left bank of the Seine. In the background can be seen the spire of the Sainte-Chapelle, and the Law Courts, while in front of the Sainte-Chapelle is the Quai des Orfèvres (Quay of the Goldsmiths), the site of the headquarters of the Paris police, well known to readers of the Maigret stories. (In the Inspector's office overlooking the river, countless interrogations were of such duration that beer and sandwiches had to be sent out for!) The Quai was severely damaged during the Commune (1871), then greatly enlarged over the period 1911–1914.

Mimi Pinson's House I. Mimi was a young dressmaker of the kind sentimentalised in Henri Murger's *Bohemian Life*. She is said to have been industrious and underfed; amorous and pleasure-loving : she is in fact a character in a story by the nineteenth-century poet, Alfred de Musset, in which she pawns her only dress to save a starving friend. Such was her popularity, however, that she was believed to have lived in this little house in Montmartre, and until it was pulled down in 1926, young girls would regularly lay bunches of flowers on the threshold in Mimi's memory.

Mimi Pinson's House II.   Another view of what used to be no 18 rue du Chevalier de la Barre : even the site is now deep under the tide of reinforced concrete. The girl leaning against the elegant lamp-post could be Mimi herself (Pinson means 'finch' — an indication that de Musset's opinion of her intellect was not a very flattering one).

The Lapin Agile. This little restaurant is still at no 4 rue des Saules, Montmartre, opposite Montmartre's own vineyard. Its trademark — a rabbit escaping from a saucepan brandishing a bottle of wine — is a visual pun : *Là peint A. Gill* ('painted by A. Gill', the artist) can also be transliterated as *lapin agile* or 'nippy rabbit'. Over the years, many leading French artists and writers dined here, some leaving pictures, sketches or poems to pay the bill.

Montmartre Windmills. The list in the Montmartre museum puts the total number at 14. All had names and legends, like the one about the Moulin de la Galette, according to which several members of the Debray family, which owned the mill, were killed resisting the Cossack invasion during the campaign of France in 1814. One was sabred to death, and pieces of his body stuck on the sails of his own mill. Only a mock-up of the Moulin de la Galette survives as the symbol of a music-hall, trading on memories of the rustic charm of old Montmartre.

Moulin de la Galette. The original 'girdle-cake mill', as it stood in the winding rue Lepic in Montmartre. Though it was already being used as a dance-hall, corn, from which the cakes were made, was still ground. The present Moulin is on a different site, and caters for a different clientele, the Debray family having finally presented it to the city of Paris. In its unsophisticated heyday, it was painted by Auguste Renoir, and offered a wide range of attractions, including a shooting gallery, roundabouts and automata.

The Moulin Rouge. The Moulin Rouge shown here, home of the can-can dancers immortalised in the paintings of Toulouse-Lautrec, was burned down just before the First World War. It had itself replaced an earlier music-hall known as 'La Reine Blanche' : a good idea of its origins is given in Jean Renoir's film *French Can-Can*. The highly-trained squads of dancers with their foaming underskirts, advancing and retreating to the wild music of Jacques Offenbach, and concluding with *le grand écart* (the splits), have given way to elaborately-staged nude revues.

Place de la Concorde.   This magnificent square was built between 1757 and 1773, to honour King Louis XV, and named successively Place Louis XV; Place de la Révolution; Place de la Concorde, and again Place Louis XV, before reverting finally to its present name, it was originally conceived as a setting for a statue of Louis XV which was destroyed during the Revolution of 1789. Here political executions were carried out during the Revolution : between 1792 and 1795, the number of people guillotined on the then Place de la Révolution — including King Louis XVI and Queen Marie-Antoinette — amounted to 1,119.

Paul Desoye (1888–1964)
Photographer reporter

Interested in all innovations of his time (the beginning of aeronautics and motor vehicles), **Paul Desoye** carried out his most important works between 1908 and 1914, — about 2,000 photographic plates (13 × 18 cm) with a heavy Gaumont 'Spidos' type camera, allowing snapshots of Paris during the *Belle Epoque*.

Publicity agencies in London and Paris used his photographs. The war stopped his activities and he never again made use of his talents. His son, **Jacques Desoye,** manager of a large photographic laboratory in Bourg-la-Reine, revealed his father's works in 1960 by producing a postcard collection.

This collection is called 'PARIS 1900', and has been distributed by **Yvon** since 1975.

J. B. Wright was born at Retford, Nottinghamshire, in 1920. Educated at King Edward VI Grammar School, Retford, and London University, he joined the Civil Service in 1939, but was soon called up into the Army. He served first in RAOC/REME, then in the Intelligence Corps in Egypt, the Western Desert, Libya, Tunisia and Eritrea. After demobilisation in 1946, he entered the Diplomatic Service, and served successively in Jerusalem, West Germany, Iraq, Taiwan, Indonesia, Cyprus, Tunisia, Vietnam, Switzerland, and in 1975 was appointed Ambassador to Ivory Coast, Upper Volta and Niger. He retired from the Diplomatic Service in 1979. He has always had a keen interest in France and the French, and since his retirement has written two books of francophone interest : *Francophone Black Africa Since Independence* and *Zaire Since Independence*. He has also contributed to a number of periodicals on a wide variety of topics, often with an Anglo–French flavour, such as a recent essay in *The Kipling Journal* on Rudyard Kipling's life-long passion for France. He also works as a translator and lecturer. In 1979, he received the award of Companion of St. Michael and St. George.

Back cover, left : *The Sacré-Coeur.* The Basilica of the Sacred Heart stands at a height of 420 feet above sea level, and completely dominates Central Paris. It was begun after a resolution had been adopted in the National Assembly endorsing a nationwide vow of humility and repentance following the disasters of the Franco-Prussian War and the Commune of 1870–1. Though the foundation stone was laid in 1875, it was not formally consecrated until 1919. It can hold a congregation of 8,000, and the tolling of its bell, La Savoyarde, is audible thirty miles away.

Back cover, right : *Rue Poulbot, Montmartre.* A typical Montmartre street, named after the artist Francisque Poulbot, who died in 1946 : the centenary of his birth was celebrated in 1979 with the issue of a stamp bearing one of his drawings of Montmartrois urchins, which became so famous that such boys were known as 'poulbots'. In 1921, Poulbot, who spent most of his life in Montmartre, founded a dispensary for these children, many of whom were orphans. He was also prominent among those seeking to defend Montmartre against the encroachments of speculative builders.